# SNAKECICLES

I hope this can bring some joy
to this dark time we are all
going through.

Happy reading!

**TIM GILGE**

ISBN for the Printed version: 979-8-566-57494-3
ISBN for the E-book version: 978-0-578-80863-5

Hunting, Trapping, Fishing, and Homeschooling
A Series of Short Stories About an Atypical
Montana Family

Printed in the United States of America.

Cover Design by 100Covers.com
Interior Design by FormattedBooks.com

*In loving memory of Katherine "Katie" Jiron, 1994–2020.*

*She passed while this book was still in progress. I wish you were able to see it done. Without you, this book would not have happened. Look forward to hearing your voice again, and you hearing mine.*

# A Message from Kent Gilge (Dad)

These stories came about as a result of the family getting together for my daughter Katie's wedding in 2014. As my four sons (Kirby, Jesse, Kody, Tim) and I were sitting around telling stories and laughing uncontrollably, number four son, Tim, said, "We need to write these down for posterity."

Everyone looked at him and agreed, as he had thought of it, that it was now his job. His brothers all kidded him about the fact that he can't spell.

Tim responded, "They have a thing called spell-check now." (Plus, an editor helps, a lot.)

I think you will agree he can tell a story.

Even though she doesn't appear much in this collection of stories, my daughter Katie is the reason this book exists. She might not have gotten into the funny kind of trouble you'll find in this book, but these stories wouldn't have been put into print without her.

# Introduction and Disclaimer from Tim Gilge (Son)

This book is a compilation of stories involving hunting, fishing, trapping, homeschooling, and any other odd tidbits that happened to come to mind. It is the partial history of a family, a great family, but a weird family by some people's standards.

These stories will be told in a semi conversational way, meaning that sometimes the tense will change, sometimes being present and sometimes being past tense, depending on the story.

We always thought every family had these stories … until we started telling them. We're kinda like the Duck Dynasty guys … without all the money, and I think they might have better beards.

My folks were the type that wouldn't let us play with toy guns when we were little. They gave us real guns.

Some things written here may be graphic and not appropriate for wimps. Some unique language may be used, but only to appropriately describe events. No laws were broken, I think. All licenses and taxes were acquired and paid. Most animals were harmed. Names may be omitted to protect the guilty.

It's important to understand that our family believes that mankind should manage and utilize flora and fauna as a given responsibility by God. Because of this, we enjoy the chase, the hook set, the hunt, and the trap.

As sportsmen, it is our duty to protect, utilize, manage, and thin game and predator populations. No cruelty was ever intended, nor planned with malice. As all good sportsmen, we endeavor the kill to be as quick and merciful as possible and utilize everything we can from the animal. Even when things did not go as planned, understand that even a bad death by man's hand is still a merciful one compared to nature's way, that is, starvation, freezing, disease, and predators, who often eat their prey alive.

You also need to understand that these stories are a by-product of many things, but a major one is being homeschooled.

This childhood was the best I could imagine, a modern Huck Finn adventure, which I think any child would be envious of.

My parents believed that daytime was for work, chores, and outdoor activities. When the sun went down, we did our homework. (Makes logical sense doesn't it). A lot of our education was acquired in the field and hands-on. We were able to see, do, and experience things most children only dream of. Biology, math, science, but my favorite was chemistry … Not all homeschoolers are like us or vice versa; we are a very diverse and free group of people.

Enough with the ideology. Let's get on with it.

Jokes have always been a mainstay in my family, young and old for as long as I can remember. We have all had hard times in life, financially, spiritually, personally, and so on. Sometimes a laugh, even at yourself can help. We also grew up on quotes from baseball superstar Yogi Berra; those quotes are called Yogi-isms.

Throughout the book, our family's favorite jokes and Yogi-isms will serve as breaks or separators to give you a breather from the wild tales contained herein.

# Tidy Whities Camouflage

On the last day of hunting season, we were searching for antelope on the prairie. My father had not yet filled his tag. It's the time of year when there are intermittent patches of snow littering the landscape, and the antelope (also called "speed goats") are already shedding their horn sheaths.

A lot of people do not know the difference between horns and antlers, so let me explain. Horns are permanent, unlike antlers, which are fully shed every year. Speed goats have horns, but with sheaths or shells, the outer part of the horn is made up of hairlike fiber, which is shed at the end of the year. Their horns typically have a single main prong that curls toward the end, with a front prong protruding. This kind of makes them look like can openers.

Up to this point on this day, we had a very hard time stalking these freakishly fast, binocular vision animals. Somehow, they always know when we are close.

My father's explanation for this was a supposed article he had read regarding animals' ability to make out human facial patterns. This topic dominated the conversation for quite a while, as you can imagine.

So there we were, driving the roads around our favorite hunting spots, when we saw a large herd of antelope. The area they occupied was owned by the Bureau of Land Management (BLM) and was as flat as God's cutting board—with one exception, a small rise of a man-made dam, making a small reservoir. The mound/dam was covered with patches of snow and dust. It did provide us with what we needed to close the distance and also some cover to break the line of sight, hide our truck, and make a stalk.

It was not a very large rise, just enough so that after walking for a while hunched down, we were forced to belly crawl to the top. It was during this crawl, about fifteen feet from the top, that my father broke out his secret weapon before we peeked over the crest.

We were crawling right next to one another when suddenly, he was gone. I stopped and looked back, only to find him digging in his jacket for something. He found it. A pair of tidy whities.

What he did next baffled me. He placed them upon his head and proceeded to crawl up the hill! Here is this grizzly mountain man with a full beard, decked out in camo and hunting gear, topped off with a white undergarment covering his face, looking out through a single leg hole with his Ruger 30-06 cradled in his arms.

Screw the stalk, this was funny! It took everything I had to keep from bursting out laughing in the middle of the crawl.

To his credit, there were patches of snow on this rise, so the color and breakup was appropriate. He has always been a frugal man and therefore, at this time in his life, would not even think of spending ten or twenty dollars on a hunting mask.

This was all too much. I was still smiling to myself when we reached the top of the rise. But low and behold, the speed goats had bolted.

They were already a long way out, trotting and quartering away. This made me smile as well since his face, now in "camouflage" was not the reason for their quick departure.

At this point, while still laying on the ground watching the goats, I am already playing out the argument he would make on the way home, which would be along the lines of, "They spooked because *I* did not have camouflage on, and they facially recognized me," or something to that end. This argument has been brought up in the past with previous renditions of the story, mostly by my father. So let me dispel this now: those animals were moving long before we were visible.

He pulled up his rifle and was watching them. I figured he was just seeing if there was a good buck in the group or perhaps where they might be heading. I did not think much of it, because my father had a 30-06 Ruger Mark I, with a fixed 3X Redfield scope, which I swear makes things zoom out instead of in. My rifle had a real 9X scope on it. I was using that scope to watch the speed goats run away, and even with my 9X, they looked tiny and I could barely make out the buck. I was glad for the rest after the stalk and did not complain.

*Boom!* My dad's gun went off.

I was right next to him and got some snow muzzle wash in my face. It made me jump since I was not expecting it at all. My first reaction was to give him a stupid look, then realizing he was still sighting downrange and his shot was deliberate, I quickly brought my rifle back up.

I found the herd, which looked like ants now, and I watched as one ant faltered, slowed, split from the herd, and fell.

Dad went back to get the truck and told me to pace off the shot. I got out to around five hundred yards before I saw the animal and in my excitement, still being a child, forgot my count and ran the rest of the way.

It was the most amazing shot I had ever seen, and maybe the best shot I will ever see, with a demagnifying fixed 3X scope, no less!

Dad had found a road that led close to us and had walked to meet me. He had taken his "camouflage" off at this point and instead donned a shit-eating grin.

We went to the downed animal together. From what we saw walking up, it had a nice curl and looked about fourteen inches long, until we rolled him over. He had already shed his other sheath. (Bet you didn't see that through your 3X, Dad).

To this day, I never go anywhere, without wearing a pair of "proper camouflage."

In the end, don't be afraid to look the fool. Sometimes you should put underwear on your head and take the long shot. Remember, most superheroes wear their underpants on the outside of their clothes.

# Sharing

Do you know why clams and oysters never share anything?

They're shellfish.

# Backseat Antelope

My brother Kody took two of his friends who had never hunted antelope out to our usual stomping grounds near Chinook, Montana. He borrowed our dad's little S-10 pickup with a topper.

You know the type: a little two-seater truck with room for one on the hump. I'm not sure who usually got the hump in your family, but if it was anything like my experiences, it was most likely the youngest brother.

The topper was one of those thin aluminum tops made from pop-can material. It also had a single small sliding window behind the middle seat. (This comes into the story later.)

After a while, they finally spotted a herd of antelope. Unfortunately, it was very flat land, so my brother had to use a form of hunting we call "running and gunning," where you drive as fast as you can to where the little speed demons are going, you bail out of the truck, sneak over the hill, and try and get some shots downrange before jumping back in to cut them off again. Works well if you know the area and terrain.

His friends had a hard time hitting these animals. A very hard time. Again and again, they would bail out, run to the fence or over the hill—*boom, boom,*

*boom*—run back, and jump back in, drive, jump out, and repeat. They soon found themselves running out of daylight and bullets. At one point, they even made a trip back into town to resupply ammo.

After a long and tiresome ordeal, one lucky shot dropped a nice buck in his tracks. Anyone who's used to hunting or has spent time with such videos on YouTube has probably seen an animal running full out and then—*bam*—nose first into a comical skidding dirt nap.

There is blood on the head, and the dramatic stop tells them it was a head-shot. Not intentional … but a headshot none the less.

My brother is beyond relieved. The antelope died in an alfalfa field next to a farm road. After some thought, my brother didn't want to process and gut the antelope there and leave an unseemly gut pile near the road, so he tells his friends to tag it but then to just grab the antelope and throw it in the back, and they'll take it down the road.

For this story, let's call the antelope "Steve," mainly so I don't have to keep writing "antelope," but I have also grown attached to this animal in the process of telling this story.

They are all bouncing along in the little S-10 when they come to a gate. Some nonresident hunters have just opened it and are politely waiting for my brother to come through before closing it. The S-10 pulls up next to the other hunters and they start chewing the fat. "Have you gotten anything? Seen any big ones?" and so on. They are in the middle of this when they notice the other hunters' banter taper off dramatically, and there's a funny look on their faces. They all appeared to be looking intently in the back of the truck topper.

My brother looks in his rearview mirror, and what does he see?

Steve.

Steve is standing up, legs splayed wide for balance, bleeding from his head, looking both confused and slightly pissed off. The banter has now died; no one is talking. Utter silence and everything is still, everyone waiting to see what Steve will do.

After just a moment, Steve decides he does not like the confined space under the topper of the S-10, so he scrambles until his feet are fully under him and starts smashing it as hard and as fast as he can with his horns. He's ripping open the topper like a World War II P-38.

One clear thought blasts through to my brother: *His footing! I must keep him from getting his footing!*

Off they fly in a flurry of gravel, leaving the other hunters gawking in the dust.

No one really knows what is going on or what to do with a pissed off, disorientated animal in the back of this truck. My brother just keeps speeding up and slowing down to keep Steve from getting his feet under him.

Did you ever wonder why their horns look like a can opener? It's because they are, and they work.

My brother is trying to think of how he's going to explain the swiss cheese topper to my dad as Steve tries to continue his assault: *Ventilation holes? Better for aerodynamics? Dad will never buy that.*

The floor of the truck bed is metal, and Steve is sliding around like a greased egg on a hot skillet.

*It's working!* thinks my brother, followed shortly by, *What in the hell do we do now?*

While all of this is going on, one of the friends decides he has to get some pictures of this, thinking to himself, *How else would anyone believe something like this?*

So where is this camera? He left it in his pack in the bed of the truck. Fortunately, it's near the front of the bed, just below the sliding window. Unfortunately, on the other side of the glass is a pissed off Steve.

He decides to risk it. He slides open the window to stick his arm through and grab the camera. At that same moment, my brother decides to go to the slow-down phase, pushing on the brakes.

Steve shoots forward into the now open window, head poking through the slider, blood spurting on their faces from Steve's head wound. Steve then decides he wants in the front seat. It must have looked roomy, and the open window was clearly an invitation. Now, there is Steve, head and horns partially through the back window and working on a shoulder enthusiastically.

The two passengers try to fight off Steve's sudden urge to join them in the front cab. My brother finally finds a place to pull off on this dirt road, and they come to a skidding stop, gravel flying, and they all bail out.

Steve no longer wants in the front seat. Since he now has his feet under him, he decides to go back to his newly acquired hobby of punching ventilation holes in the topper with renewed vigor.

The three boys are now standing outside the S-10, covered in blood, hair, and smelling of sagebrush. (Antelope smell like sagebrush—not a bad smell actually.) They are now watching as the truck rocks back and forth, with

Steve venting his rage on the confining aluminum of the topper. They have a moment to think.

"The bullet must have grazed him in the back of the head and knocked him out cold," one of the friends comments.

"Well, he's not out cold now!" the other replies.

They carefully retrieve their rifles from the truck cab and go to the back of the truck near the tailgate. Kody looks at his friends and gives them the nod. You know the nod. The one that says, "Hey, I'm going to drop the tailgate, let this guy out, and you guys shoot it, okay?" It was a very complex and nuanced nod.

The tailgate drops, Steve flies out like a bat out of hell. Remember, he did just have a recent head injury, and I do not think using his head as a can opener had any positive effects either. Steve made a valiant, but drunken-like dash. He even dodged a few bullets, but in the end, he made it back to our home and the meat pole.

The truck topper no longer works for keeping water or anything else out and has been retired to our backfield, where it sits to this day as a reminder of Steve's resurrection.

Moral of the story: It ain't dead till it's on the meat pole, and if you borrow something and break it, you better have a good story to go with it.

# Yogi-ism

"I never said most of the things I said."

# A Rocky Trip Down Rock Creek

Salmon flies are gigantic stone flies that live, as juveniles, in rocky stream bottoms. A few days of the year they come to the surface and hatch into adults. This initiates a fantastic trout feeding frenzy. Rock Creek has one of the largest hatches, and things go crazy when it comes to fishing. The hatch usually occurs around the first week of June, and depending on the year, there may be large amounts of melting snow swelling the river.

Knowing that the hatch was about to start, my brother Kody and his good friend Ben decided they were going to be there at all costs. They studied a remote stretch of river that they had never been on and that appeared difficult for other fishermen to get to. It looked great from the Google Earth photos, as it always does.

They outfitted themselves with high-priced fly rods, reels, and vests. They each purchased their fly-fishing pontoon boats. (Think a hybrid of a tube and a boat). These boats are designed to sit with your feet in the water. However, after some very rough back-of-the-napkin calculations, they decided to modify them.

They bought extensions for the seats and picked out some oars. These extensions lifted the seats to the point of almost standing. They believed this would give them casting and viewing advantages. But they didn't get extensions for the oars.

Word finally reached them that some salmon flies had been spotted on the creek. The modifications and equipment were hastily assembled the night before, never tried or tested, but they were confident they were going to work.

Kody and Ben arrived in the town nearby Rock Creek on Saturday morning and started driving to their put-in location. The creek seemed to be running a bit high and fast, but looked manageable, or so they thought.

It just happened that it was the weekend of high school graduations, so all the locals were with family or celebrating. This is a popular river, and while it should have been overflowing with local fishermen, they had the river to themselves. They were ecstatic.

As they arrived at their launch point, they saw thousands of three-inch salmon flies lying around on rocks and trees and could hear large fish slurping them off the river. Not only were there no other fishermen, but they had hit the peak of the hatch.

Crisp clean air and the sound of rushing water drew them like a magnet to the river as they hauled their rafts down through the brush. Ahead of them was what they thought would be a leisurely ten-mile float, which would take most of the day.

The water was moving fast, but they were on a straight stretch, so they eagerly proceeded. Kody pushed out first. Despite his enthusiastic attempt, the current immediately pushed him back to shore and into the thorny brush that covered the riversides. This tangled him up. Meanwhile, Ben pushed out into the river a little further upstream and was able to clear the brush and make it around the bend while Kody untangled himself. Ben got a couple of hundred yards ahead of Kody, got his rod ready, and went around the next bend.

Immediately around that bend, and just out of sight, was a massive log jam. Ben hit the log jam and scrambled from his raft to the top and somehow managed to save his raft and started to pull it to the side. He initially saved his fly rod; however, in the rough crossing to the shore, he lost it to the fast-moving waters.

Not five minutes into the trip, they were down one rod and other essential equipment.

Kody came around the same bend, and it was at this moment he realized that his oars were a hindrance. The oars were so short they barely reached the water … because of the seat extensions. With no way to control himself, Kody did the same thing Ben did and smashed into the log jam. Ben was there for him and helped him pull everything to the bank.

They portaged around the log jam and took a moment to assess the situation. Fish were feeding frantically, so they stopped on a gravel bar to get into the action with the sole surviving rod. The fishing was amazing. Kody and Ben took turns catching one trout after another—sixteen- to twenty-inch browns, rainbows, and cutthroats.

They decided to get back out on the river. They reasoned that they had the whole day ahead of them, a long way to go, and they were certain that larger fish awaited them downstream, where nobody usually fished.

Peering downstream, the river swirled around a cliff, and they could see white water. They took some time preparing and getting ready, strapping things down, making sure pockets were buttoned, tackle boxes secured, and mentally pumping themselves up for what they knew was about to be a rocky trip.

Ben went first and got slammed into the cliff during the turn. Kody had the last surviving rod in a plastic holder, secured with a Velcro strap on the side of the pontoon. Kody was a little behind Ben and had seen him slam into the cliff. Right before he went into the rapids, Kody thought to himself, *If I hit the cliff as Ben did, I'll break my rod.*

As Kody was speeding into the thick of it, he undid the Velcro strap on the rod but kept it in the plastic holder, thinking, *If I have to, I can yank my rod out and hold it to keep it from getting snapped.*

Kody cleared the cliff with a sigh of relief, and—relaxing too soon, as he turned around the bend—he went straight into the rapids on the other side comprised of four, three-foot drops. He hit them in fast succession, each building energy. The last was bigger than the others and spiked him into the air. The raft rocketed into the sky about five feet and flipped end over end. All he remembered was seeing the sky and then the tip of his fly rod drop below the surface about ten feet downstream.

The water was moving fast, so he dragged his feet as much as he could, hoping out of sheer desperation to snag something as the river ripped him past the location of his rod. No luck. He lost his rod, vest, his set of oars, and fly box, as well as his hat and sunglasses.

About a mile further downstream, he got back on his raft. A little while later, they regrouped, and working together, they were able to make it to the shore. They took stock, They were now down two rods, a vest, two fly boxes, one set of oars, sunglasses, lunch, and many other supplies. They passed additional un-factored-in tributaries, which were adding swollen masses of runoff water to the creek, making it faster and more dangerous the further down they went.

*These were not on Google Maps!* They thought to themselves.

Now they were just trying to make it back alive.

They reached the next stretch, and Ben snagged on a shoreline. There was a big sweeping tree that he tried to paddle around. However, because the oars did more harm than good, they turned him right around. The tree hit him in the back of the head and knocked him off the raft, which promptly overturned as well. Kody helped his sputtering companion, with a fresh head wound, back to his raft, which was now missing its oars as well.

Huge trout slashed the surface in every direction. And all they could do was watch and try to survive.

A few moments later, Kody was thrown into a large log/brush pile. The pile had large logs jammed up in all directions, but it was also intertwined with the thorny brush from the riversides, like an antitank barrier covered in barbwire. It is not something you enjoy colliding with at any velocity. He became pretty torn up, and his shirt was in tatters. Despite significant shrinkage of the pontoons due to many punctures, they shot downstream. Without oars, they were bouncing off rocks and trees like pinballs.

They finally arrive at the landing, their leisurely "all day" trip completed in just over one hour. Keep in mind that at this point, Kody and Ben had nothing left to show that they were actually fishermen. Clothes shredded, covered in wounds, bloody, and lacking energy, they pulled the flat pontoons all the way onto shore, using their last bit of energy. Then they collapsed.

After a while, they recovered enough to stand, staring at the dozens of monstrous, hungry trout slamming and gulping flies up and down the river just feet in front of them. All they had left were the deflated rafts.

After a short discussion, they decided to leave those where they lay. The river took everything else from them; someone else could have the rafts.

They walked to the river's edge and emptied the spare change and gravel that remained in their pockets and sent it all flying into Rock Creek as one last offering to join two high-priced Sage fly rods, most of the gear and tackle, hats, clothes—and all of their dignity.

# Mugged

A slug is working his way down a dark alley in Detroit when two turtles emerge out of the darkness and mug him.

Someone hears the commotion and calls the cops.

The cops and paramedics come and tend to the slug. They then ask the slug to tell them what happened.

The slug says, "I don't know. It all happened so fast."

# The End of a Valiant Muskrat

This story begins, as most good hunting stories do, with a father dragging his lazy son out of bed well before sunrise.

While driving out to our hunting grounds, my father told me that we needed a muskrat for one of my brother's taxidermy mounts. It was going to be a side piece to another mount he was doing with a bobcat.

Sunrise is prime time for spotting moving animals. After glassing the sky-line for quite a while, my young eyes grow weary. It was at that moment that I caught movement out of the corner of my eye. What did I see in the middle of the road to my disbelief? A fat muskrat hauling butt down the middle of the dirt road from right to left.

(I later found out that this is common. During dry seasons, muskrats will migrate to new water sources, sometimes over many miles of land.)

"Dad, Dad, look!" I proclaimed.

My father frantically searched the skyline, believing I had found some antelope.

"No! On the road!" I said.

As my dad finally grasped what I was trying to convey, he dropped his binoculars and spotted the same strange scene I was beholding. We frantically dug around, trying to find a weapon besides our high-powered hunting rifles that would dispatch the little creature without utterly obliterating its hide. Hunting rifles should not be used for small rodents—not if you want to find any part of it afterward.

The only thing at hand was a small, spring-loaded contraption used to quickly clip on the end of a rifle as a bipod. With its two black plastic legs and small spring, it was about a foot in length and weighed slightly more than a leaded feather.

We set off to intercept the furry traveler. My father headed out left in front of the wee creature, while I headed right and behind him to cut off any escape route. Time seemed to slow down. It seemed like I could read the muskrat's facial expressions and his thoughts as clear as my own. I will do my best to interpret what I witnessed.

The muskrat threw on the brakes upon seeing my father with the deadly plastic wand in hand. He skidded to a stop, gravel flying in every direction.

*Oh no*, he seemed to say.

Quickly, he enacted his fallback escape route, the drainage ditch on the side of the road. He turned right and in one mighty jump, bounded headfirst into the ditch. But alas, it was dry. He bounced and tumbled into the dusty ditch, a cloud of dust rising around his still form. At that moment, he seemed to be processing this ill turn of events, the same way a star gymnast stays down for a few moments longer than needed after failing to stick the dismount.

Dad stepped down into the ditch and was fast approaching the musk-rat, who had, at this point, regained his wits and hopped to all fours, glancing around and assessing his tactical situation. It was grim. He was now in a ditch, my father in front. He turned, and I was there behind him. Something changed in his eyes. He turned back to my father. There was no longer flight, only fight!

He braced himself and, I imagine, said a prayer. With his action decided, he acted. He needed height to get to the same level as his pursuers. He quickly jumped to a boulder on his left, then bounded upon another to the right and another, gaining altitude.

Dad was advancing slowly, more cautiously now. As the muskrat reached the highest rock, he stopped. The two foes squared off. Being a spectator at this point, I sat back and watched it all.

Much like the Spartans facing the Persians at Thermopylae, the swamp rat rose on his rear legs and roared in his final defiance as best he could. Being a twenty-ounce animal, he sounded more like a very quiet door hinge, but in my mind, it was a roar.

It was clear he would not go quietly into the night.

With a nod, my father accepted his challenge and advanced upon his raised position on the boulder, which was only about a foot and a half high. Dad lifted his small, blunt, plastic gladius, and the muskrat leaped from his rock, head turning sideways, jaws opening for what was his target: my father's jugular.

His fur waved in the air—a hairy missile on a dedicated course.

But he did not achieve his goal. He might have been as high as my father's waist when the gladius fell. With one quick tap to his nose, the valiant muskrat fell. Time resumed its pace, and my story ends.

I believe that we should all hope to have such bravery at the end of our ditch, to jump at the throat of what may be our end.

# Animal Control

A man walks out in his front yard and sees a gorilla climb up into his tree. He's not sure what to do, so he calls the local game warden.

The game warden shows up and assesses the situation. He goes back to his truck and comes back with a mean-looking little dog, some handcuffs, and a pistol. He gives the guy the handcuffs and the pistol.

He tells the guy, "Okay, here's the plan. I'm going to climb up that tree and knock that gorilla down to the ground. When he hits the ground, that little dog is going to attack and lock onto his crotch like a vice grip. That's when you run up and slap the handcuffs on him while he's trying to get him off."

The man asks, "What about the pistol?"

The warden replies, "Well, the plan is that I'm going to climb up and knock that gorilla out of the tree, but if the gorilla gets the best of me and knocks me out of the tree, you shoot that little dog."

# The Mountain Man with a Backseat Coyote

My father always wanted to be a mountain man, even from his youth. His problem was that he grew up in Chicago. He always felt he was a geographically misplaced person. He would take any opportunity to fish when he could. Then, when the opportunity presented itself, he went to school in Montana so he could study biology.

In the process, he met and married my mother while attending college. My mother and father, after moving around with my dad's postings with the Fish and Game Department, ended up moving to the Hi-Line of Montana to put down roots.

When he moved to Montana, one of his goals was to learn how to trap coyotes. One fateful year, he teamed up with a trapping partner who had trapped with his father since he was a boy and was very knowledgeable. After learning how to catch coyotes, my father tried to learn a little bit about killing them. He had always shot his coyotes with a .22 pistol, but the blood made a mess, and fur washing was tedious. His new partner showed him a bloodless technique. You just simply break their necks. This fit right into my dad's idea of what a mountain man would do.

His mentor demonstrated this technique for my father one time on a coyote. He rapped the dog sharply on the nose with a stick and it went out cold for about five seconds. He then pounced on the coyote, grabbed its muzzle while firmly holding it by the neck. A quick backward push on the muzzle and—*snap*—it was over.

Dad's turn came with the next coyote. He got the rapping on the nose part right, then jumped on him, grabbed the muzzle, and twisted back the head. No snap. About this time, the coyote came out of his dazed phase, and the wrestling match began. My father learned that without the "snap" part of the technique, you soon have a fully awake coyote in your hands that you really can't let go of.

Sometimes Dad was on top, and sometimes the coyote was on top. He finally had to let go and get back quickly, none the worse except for about a hundred fleas all over him. That one was shot ... more tedious washing.

He figured he needed to practice on something smaller. He caught a fox. This ended in the same result, except fox have about a thousand times more fleas than coyotes. That one also was shot, then both received a chemical bath to kill the biblical legion of fleas that they now shared.

The next effort came when he caught a mink in a trap. Usually, these sets are made so the animal drowns, but this one became tangled up before it hit the water. Dad figured this would be a smaller animal to try out the old neck-breaking routine. He just needed something small enough to perfect this technique, right? He grabbed the mink by the neck, put his hand under the chin, and pushed back. The problem was that mink really don't have a muzzle or a neck, and they are fast as lightning. The mink latched onto his thumb with a vise grip. Dad was hopping around with the mink still attached to the staked trap and his thumb as the stream rushed around them.

My brother Jesse was right there, so Dad told him to grab a stick and whack him on the head really hard. So he did. And as you would expect, all it did was drive the needlelike teeth down to the bone. The vise grip turned up a crank; he couldn't let go of the mink and couldn't get him off. He tried to hold the mink underwater to drown it, but the mink was apparently getting oxygen directly from my father's blood, as he tells it, and the mink would not succumb.

(More likely is that mink have amazing lung capacities and can hold their breath for a long time.)

He switched to philosophical and logical arguments; however, the mink was neither moved nor swayed. He told my brother to go get a pair of pliers, he wedged them in between the jaws, and finally, he pried his bloody thumb out.

*At least there aren't any fleas*, he thought. That pretty much ended his experimentation with the neck dispatch technique until a new situation arose.

* * *

Several years go by, and my father has mostly forgotten about his various attempts at practicing the bloodless neck-break technique.

When the two oldest boys were about four and six, my father decided to introduce them to trapping on my coyote line. They were pretty much relegated to sitting in the backseat and watching to minimize human scent around the traps. The trapping vehicle at the time was a small Mazda hatchback.

As they approached one of the sets, my father noticed that he had caught a large male coyote. Having given up on the neck-breaking technique, he loaded his pistol and shot him in the brain just above the eye as the boys observed through the car windows. He rebaited the set and threw the coyote in a black plastic bag to contain the blood and, more importantly, the fleas.

He raised the hatchback and threw in the bag, not giving it a second thought. He then drove to the edge of the ridge to check another set way down in a draw. He told the boys to stay put and that he would be back in a minute. Nothing was in the set, and he returned to the car to find two wide-eyed boys staring straight ahead at him.

In unison, he heard them say, "I saw that coyote stick his head out of the bag."

He remembers thinking, *Those boys have quite an imagination.*

As he put the car in reverse and looked in the rearview mirror, he stopped cold as the head and shoulders of this large coyote was sitting up only inches above my brothers' heads.

The coyote's head was all bloody, tongue hanging out, panting, and very much alive. He shut off the engine and told the boys to freeze. He quietly opened the door and ran around to the hatchback, opened it up, grabbed the coyote by the back of the head, pinned it to the ground, and swiftly broke its neck. He says he hardly remembers doing it.

My father realized he had missed one key ingredient in developing the technique of neck-snapping, which was the gallon of adrenaline that flows through you when your children are in harm's way. He doesn't think he wants to try that again. And now, the Mazda had fleas in it as well.

# Yogi-ism

"In theory, there is no difference between theory and practice. In practice there is."

Jesse and Dani Gilge, with their children Reece and Brynn

# An Un-bear-able Incident

Our story begins on the way to the sixth birthday party for Brynn, daughter of Jesse and Dani Gilge.

The SUV was packed with six excited and eager party guests ranging in ages from four to nine. The group was running late, so Dani hurriedly wrangled the kids into the vehicle and took off. There was the typical chatter, horseplay, and other nonsense going on that you'd imagine from a rig full of kids, but to Dani in the driver's seat, all seemed well.

In the furthest back seat sat two boys. Reece (eight), the older brother of Brynn, and his best friend Liam. The two boys were bugging the girls in the seats in front of them and generally carrying on when Dani slowed down for a red light. Now, keep in mind this is a Gilge vehicle, ready for anything …

What rolls out from beneath their seat, but a can of bear spray. This was from a recent hiking trip Jesse took in bear country, and it must have fallen out of his pack upon his return.

What happened next is not one hundred percent clear, but through questioning different sources over time, it's believed that there might have been some peer pressure involved by previously mentioned best friend. Perhaps a double-dog dare or the equivalent.

What is clear is that Reece removed the safety mechanism and proceeded to activate the bear spray. He did not know it was pointed directly at him, and the shot landed on his lower face and neck. Because he felt the immediate and painful repercussions of his action so quickly, it was a very short spray.

Dani heard a yell, then a scream before her eyes started watering, and she began coughing as well. In what was now a chorus of screaming and yelling, she turned left on a red light across an intersection and found a safe place to pull off the road and try to figure out what was going on.

Around the same time, my brother Jesse is on an important web meeting when he gets a phone call. He silences it and sees it's from Dani, so he texts back,

Jesse - *On a call. What's up?*

Dani - *Emergency!!*

Jesse gets off the meeting and calls Dani back right away, and when she answers, there's screaming and crying, he can barely hear Dani, but he hears "bear spray" and "gas station." Believing he knows what gas station they are at, Jesse rushes to find his keys, but he can't. (They are in the back yard after falling from his pants pockets during a campfire the previous night.)

He rips the house apart, finally gives up, and since the gas station is only about a mile away, he decides to run it. He sprints all the way to the gas station only to not find them. He calls Dani's parents, who were able to get the location of the correct gas station and are on the way there. He sprints the mile back to the house, and despite being in very good shape, he is out of breath when he asks the neighbors to borrow their car, which they graciously allow.

The car skids to a stop at the gas station Dani found. Before it fully stops, the doors open, and kids are tumbling and jumping out, the noxious fumes right on their heels.

Jesse had been trying to call, but Dani was trying to deal with the chaos. When she answers, she just keeps repeating, "Shell on Bowles and Kipling!"

Dani sees that all of the kids are okay now that they are outside, except for Reece, who was most definitely *not* okay.

Dani tells the kids to put one hand on the car and stay there. She puts Liam (the oldest) in charge as she runs into the store to buy some water. Dani's parents arrive and start helping with the other kids.

Jesse pulls into the gas station to find a bunch of kids standing around the car with their hands on it crying, the in-laws consoling them, while Dani is pouring water over Reece's head.

Water takes the pain away briefly, and he was also comforted by being directly in front of the air conditioner blowing straight in his face.

Jesse is running inside to buy bottle after bottle of water, but at three dollars a bottle, he was doing the math in his head as to how close they were going to be to a needing a second mortgage.

At one point, on the fifth or sixth trip into the store, one of the three employee's sitting behind the desk lazily says something snarky, like "That's not going to work man," but it was the only thing working. Not a single passerby, employee, or customer offered to help during this entire event, which was quite sad.

But Reece was a trooper. Jesse told him they needed to pour the water directly into his eyes, so Reece tipped his head back and forced his eyes open even while crying.

While the water was pouring, he felt much better, but when the water ran out, it was instant pain. Zero to one hundred within seconds.

In the brief moments between screaming and crying, he was apologizing for ruining Brynn's birthday party. Even in immense pain, he was still worried about his little sister and was trying to apologize.

After about the fiftieth bottle of water, they were able to get him back to the house to use the hose for a constant stream of water. Reece asked if they could pour water on his face in the car during the ride, which Jesse said, "Of course, buddy!"

(I don't think our dad would have been so kind. He would have made us ride in the back to keep the seats dry.)

After forty-five minutes or so, everything calmed down. However, most of the occupants of the car asked Jesse some very pointed questions as to what was in his car before he could drive them home. They seemed to be concerned there might be some more spray stashed around, some even performing some cursory inspections and searches before they would get in.

I think that there are many lessons to be learned from this story:

- Don't allow peer pressure to affect you; nothing good has ever come of it.
- Don't leave bear spray in the car.

- Invest in bottled water companies, because that profit margin is insane.

But I think most importantly, if you ruin a birthday party, ruin it so well that it ends up in a book, and the retelling makes eyes water even without pressurized capsaicin.

# Inmates

A guy ends up in a federal penitentiary and is just starting to get acquainted with his new cellmate when someone down the cellblock hollers out, "Seventeen!"

Everyone on the cellblock breaks out in laughter.

A little while later, he hears an echoed "Twenty-six" from down the hall, and everybody's chuckling.

He can't take it any longer, so he asks his cellmate, "What is going on?"

The cellmate replies, "We've all been in here so long that we've heard all the same jokes a million times. So to save time, we agreed to just assign a number to our jokes."

"Oh, I see," the prisoner replies.

A little while later, he hears someone holler out, "Forty-two!" and not a single inmate laughs.

The new prisoner asks, "What's the deal?"

His cellmate replies, "Oh, that guy just doesn't know how to tell a joke."

# Pepe Le Pew Too

My childhood memories are permeated with the constant odor of skunk. You see, skunk essence is used in high-end perfume, and my father had found a buyer that would pay handsomely for it. It also helped that it could be used for lure-making for coyotes and foxes.

Our only family vehicle when I was a kid had to serve for hunting, fishing, and trapping, as well as family transportation. We got so used to the smell of skunk that we didn't notice it after a while. A friend mentioned one time that they never even had to turn around in the pew in church when our family arrived.

Everyone would just look at each other and say, "Oh, the Gilges are here."

Dad was out of town for a day, and so my brothers Jesse and Kody coerced our mother to drive them out to check the trap line. They were still young enough that Dad would not allow them to take a gun along unless he was with us. Mom was not big on guns at this point, so she wouldn't let them bring one either, but at least they got to go, so they were not complaining. I don't know how they thought they were going to deal with anything they caught, however.

Mom drove them in our little station wagon to check the first set, which was just over a flooded ditch next to a little culvert entering a small field. The two brothers got out, and Mom stayed in the car. They couldn't see the set from the top of the road because of tall grass, so they crossed the ditch by walking on the nearby culvert. Not until they were halfway across could they see what was in the trap just three feet from the car, and what a discovery they had found: a skunk!

They yelled and gestured at Mom to just gun it and keep going as they ran the rest of the way across. The skunk was taken by surprise and given multiple targets. It had just a split second of indecision, which was all that it needed to finally decided on the two brothers, most likely because it was a clear shot and the car was behind some grass and slightly over the embankment.

It took a shot and gave them a spray as they went by, missed them mostly, but you know what they say: "Close only counts in horseshoes and skunk spray," or something like that.

Now the brothers were faced with a dilemma. They could not get back to the car where Mom currently was without going back across the same culvert and line of fire that the skunk had now ranged and zeroed in on. They doubted he would miss a second time. The skunk was between them and the car, and they didn't have anything to kill the skunk with.

They told Mom to turn the car around and come back the way they had come. This would give them another way to get to the car downstream without passing right next to the pissed off pew-pew machine. Mom hit the gas and got by it as quickly as possible. Unfortunately, it was not fast enough.

By this time, the skunk was agitated and loaded for bear. He nailed the driver's side of the car with a full load on this pass. Mom said it was like going through a car wash.

They had to wait for Dad to get back before they could dispatch the little monster, as Mom would not shoot it. The story was that they washed the car every day for a month before the smell settled down. Dad said it took the clear coat off the paint on the driver's side.

\* \* \*

Another time, we were trapping gophers in a field across the road from our house. The destructive little rodents had almost destroyed the neighbor's field. Since our neighbors had horses and horses can break legs in gopher holes, Dad had given us some small traps to use and showed us where and how to set them to help the neighbor out. We came upon one larger hole, and Dad warned us not to set a trap there because he could tell a skunk was using it.

Dad was gone for a couple of days, and we laid out our line. That hole looked so inviting, and we were sure we saw gopher tracks going down into it, and besides, *What does Dad know anyway?*

The next day, we came back, and there was a big skunk in the trap. Dad was not back yet, so we were not allowed to carry a gun. We knew we would be in trouble if Dad came back and the evidence wasn't gone, so we came up with a plan. We would just throw rocks and sticks at the skunk until we killed it, then take it far away and bury it. Needless to say, all we did was irritate the skunk until he let loose on all of us, head to toe, the skunk got good coverage, and coat thickness as well.

There was now no way to hide the evidence. Eyes watering and coughing, we slogged our way home, trying to come up with a good story, which we never did. Mom smelled us way down the driveway, she came out of the house and made us strip down one hundred yards away. She hung our clothes in the trees and hosed us down with every cleaner known to man.

We didn't get in that much trouble from Dad. I think he saw how miserable we were after the military-level biohazard scrubbing Mom gave us.

He just said, "You learn a lesson?"

We mumbled some platitude, like "Yes, sir."

But looking back, I think the only lesson we learned was to get our hands on a gun when we checked traps.

# Princess Frog

A very old man from the rest home is taking his morning walk with his cane when, right at his feet, he sees a frog.

Amazingly, the frog starts to talk with the voice of a young woman. "Excuse me, sir! I know I do not currently look like it, but I'm really a beautiful princess, and if you kiss me, I'll transform and consummate your wildest dreams!"

The old man bends down and picks up the frog and puts it in his breast pocket and continues his slow trek.

The frog works its way back up out of the shirt pocket and speaks again: "Sir! I do not think you heard me. I'm really a beautiful princess. All you have to do is kiss me, and I'll transform and consummate all of your wildest dreams!"

The old man stops and looks down at the frog, "I heard you the first time," he says. "But at my age, I think I'd rather have a talking frog."

# An Elk Hunting Mad Momma

My mother has a thing about forked sticks. If for some reason the topic comes up, let's say around the fire cooking marshmallows, you will be treated to this story.

Once a year, hunting tags for special animals or areas are drawn. My father would always enter both himself and my mother for elk tag drawings. Early in their marriage, my mother drew a very coveted elk tag for a very good area. My father was very excited. I do not even know if my mother knew she had entered the drawing …

The day finally comes, and my dad set the plan.

"We'll get up a few hours before dawn and head out. We should get there in time to set up and be on them right at sunrise."

Mom's interpretation of this was, *We can eat breakfast together! We will finally have time to talk on the way out there, and then we can sit and have a romantic time watching the sunrise.*

The morning comes, and at the crack of way before dawn, Dad wakes Mom and gets her out of bed way before Mom had envisioned, she notices he is fully dressed and starts loading the last of the gear.

"B-b-but what about breakfast?" my mother says.

Dad responded in his typical fashion with, "If you wanted breakfast, you should have woke up when I did. No time. Get dressed and I'll meet you in the car."

Mom is now flustered.

The drive is a long one, and Dad tries to use this time to give Mom instructions and hunting tips. As Mom likes to talk a lot, he particularly focused her understanding on not talking during the stalk. This instruction would become problematic later.

Mom is now frustrated.

They start sneaking in before daybreak and spot a few elk heading into the trees at sunrise.

Mom keeps trying to talk and ask questions; Dad keeps shushing her.

Apparently, it worked, because they walked right into the middle of a herd of almost one hundred elk. They didn't know this at the time, however.

Mom thinks, *Oh he wants no talking does he? Well, I'll show him ... I'll give him the cold shoulder of a lifetime!*

Mom is now mad. *Here we are, freezing, no breakfast, no talking. I can't believe he told me "no talking," like I don't know how to talk on a hunt. He says words all the time while hunting. Now the sun is up, really romantic ... I'll just shoot this elk, and he can drag it out of here. Then I still won't talk to him. Ha, that'll show him.*

At about the same time, my oblivious dad is thinking, *Lois sure has been quiet. That's nice.*

Dad gave Mom his heavy 30-06, which he never let Mom shoot before because he felt she would never fire a second shot after getting thumped by it the first time.

They sneak into the thick junipers and pine trees to sit down. As the sun rises, suddenly an elk appears standing on the hillside sixty yards away. Mom struggles to lift the heavy rifle and aim.

Dad thinks, *Wait, no ... She can't hold the gun steady! The barrel's swinging in circles! She needs a rest. Yes, a shooting stick will help! Uh ... there! Right there ... a forked stick right there in front of her!*

He grabs the forked stick, what most hunters would refer to as a "shooting stick," and tries to slip it under the stock of the rifle while she is just about to pull the trigger ...

Mom is distracted by this. *What the ...? Why in the world is he shoving a stick at me? Leave me alone! I've got him, I've got him!*

Mom rebuffed all my father's attempts to get the stick under the rifle.

*Why won't she take the stick?! Take the stick!*

My mother is struggling to get Dad out of the way,

*I'm trying to shoot this elk, and I don't want a stick! What am I going to do with a stick? Get that stick out of my face!*

Mom is now beyond confused, frustrated, and mad.

The struggle intensifies in mute silence as the pro-stick side tries to use a combination of what appears to be a mix of sign language and some sort of ancient form of slow-motion Egyptian dancing to communicate his enthusiasm about the stick.

The anti-stick side finally has had enough and gets ready to shoot. In a fit of building rage, her gloved finger squeezes a little too hard, particularly upon the trigger.

*Boom!*

The gun goes off into the ground three feet in front of them, spraying pine needles into the air. The 30-06 recoil knocks her hat off.

The area erupts with all the elk they didn't see when they walked in.

This is one of those rare moments when they were both thinking the same thing.

*She needs to get another round in!*

*I need to get another round in!*

Dad tries to help Mom get another shell in the chamber, but the round stovepipes and is stuck; the bolt is not moving. Both are furiously digging at the bolt as elk practically run around and almost over them. By the time they can get another round in the chamber, all the elk are around the bend.

Dad yells, "We can catch them!"

"What?" my mother replies.

Dad grabs Mom's hand and pulls her straight up the side of a steep mountain in a full run. As Mom tells it, about a mile, in hopes of cutting the elk off, to no avail. No elk was shot that day.

Mom is now out of breath, exhausted, sweaty, she has had no breakfast, and this day has not gone anywhere close to her romantic expectation. She had been prodded and shushed, so she is quite and (I might add) understandably angry.

My father, who was focused on the hunt and elk up to this point, had not noticed the rage building up in his disheveled wife next to him.

On the hike out, Mom decided to break the no-talking rule. The walkout wasn't quiet by far.

# Stranded

A man is stranded alone on an island for twenty years. Upon being discovered by a random boat and waiting for the rescue helicopter to arrive, the man asks the boat crew, "Would you like a tour of the island?"

The boat crew agrees, being amazed that he has survived all this time.

The man shows them his house that he built and lived in for twenty years. He shows them his outhouse, his shower, and his larder.

He points to a distant hill that has two buildings and says, "The building on the right is my church."

As he continues walking, the boat crew stops him and asks, "What's the other building next to it?"

The man stops and says, "Oh, that's the church I used to go to."

Tim Gilge and Kent Gilge

Jesse, Kirby, and Kody Gilge

Snakes …

Kody and Jesse Gilge.

# Snakecicles

Catching snakes was a big part and a staple of our youthful days. But the best day was when we graduated from garter and bull snakes to rattlesnakes. Dad trained us in proper safety protocol, and when he thought we were ready, we got to tag along.

Most snake dens visited in the spring and fall yielded no more than a dozen or so, but I remember an epic day when we found a whole hillside full of dens. It was a warm spring day, and the den openings were covered with snakes soaking up the afternoon sun. When it's cold, the snakes are relatively lethargic, but these snakes were active and aggressive.

The catching technique involves one person sneaking up on the den and then rushing into the middle of them before they can get down the hole. The snakes are grabbed with four-foot tongs and thrown to a place away from the hole toward the roundup crew. Sometimes you throw them up, down, or over to the guys below.

This leaves the roundup or "can crew" watching snakes falling from the heavens all around them. They are then gathered up and placed in a fifty-gallon garbage can. We went from den to den, and in several hours, we had collected more than one hundred snakes, filling two garbage cans.

We only took the ones longer than four feet and let the little ones go. They were so aggressive that when they were grabbed with the tongs and lifted in the air you could see a mist of venom shooting into the air from their gaping mouths and fangs.

We could barely drag the cans up to the Suburban at the top of the hill. We tied down the lids and loaded them into the back. As we stood around recounting the catch and letting our heart rates subside, we all started noticing we were itching, and our eyes burned.

We soon realized that all that venom in the air had covered us like rattlesnake pepper spray. We quickly washed off with water bottles, and that helped a lot.

We put our gear away and loaded into the Suburban to head home.

The deafening rattle behind us was so loud that you could almost feel it in your teeth. It was an eerie feeling riding along with the hundred-plus live rattlesnakes in the third seat. As we bounced along down the washboard road, I remember Dad saying, "If we roll this Suburban, we better hope we all die from the impact."

The big plastic drum's lid suddenly seemed far too lose. That was a long drive home on gravel roads.

We normally chop heads at the catch site, but this was too many to deal with there, so we called a friend who owned a slaughterhouse and had a walk-in freezer that was thirty below zero. We asked if we could freeze the snakes in the drum over the weekend and he agreed.

We retrieved the snakesickles on Monday and let them thaw. Some of the snakes in the middle had half their bodies totally frozen solid, but the other half of their body was still alive and wiggling. Those we had to decapitate. I guess that's why they den up underground for the winter. Rattlesnake insulation is impressive.

(Maybe that's why it is called "R-value"?)

My brother Jesse skinned, stretched, and tanned them all on that run— quite the process.

Typically, you behead them, taking care with the head and disposing of it safely. Then you skin them, starting at the stump of the neck, using scissors down the belly. Any kind would do, but if you can get your hands on your Mom's good sewing scissors, I promise it's worth the risk and effort.

Once they are skinned, you will get the best result from fleshing them, scraping off all the attached tissue and fat from the rib portions, generally. You then stretch and staple them to a large board or plywood to dry for a day or so. Then, using a mixture of rubbing alcohol and glycerin that is applied with a paintbrush two to four times throughout a couple of days, you can preserve the skin and scales, keeping them malleable.

Jesse made over one thousand dollars on that batch. Nothing quite like spending frozen snake money.

# Reptile Problems

The medical condition a chameleon has when he
is unable to change colors anymore:

reptile dysfunction.

Lois Gilge: Our saintly mother, who is still mostly
sane after homeschooling five children.

# Our Poor, Poor Mother

Here are a few short-short stories, just to give an idea of what our mother had to put up with.

After my parent's wedding, Dad asked her where she wanted to go for the honeymoon.

She made the mistake of saying, with lovey-dovey eyes, "Anywhere … as long as I'm with you."

So my father took her fishing out in a swampland of nothing but mosquitoes, leeches, and misery for a week. But hey, at least she was with him, right?

A lesson for you ladies marrying a Gilge. Make sure your idea of an ideal honeymoon lines up with theirs. Chances are that they do not.

\* \* \*

For one of their anniversaries, Dad bought her a rifle. He then promptly left her at the house to go test out the rifle with a little coyote hunting. It tested out great and is still in the family. Why my dad was allowed back in the house after that, however, remains a mystery. His defense is that she didn't get him anything.

To this day my mother still refers to it as her rifle, although I honestly do not know if she has even used it.

\* \* \*

My older brothers somehow managed to get their hands on a book with valuable info, including how to make napalm. Knowledge is nothing without action. One of them ran into the house and told my mother she must see this cool thing they did. Excited, he leads her by the hand out to the driveway, which was completely engulfed in raging waist-high flames.

The other boys are standing around with large smiles, taking pride in a job well done.

My mother, trying to remain calm and not freak out amid this inferno, calmly says, "That's great boys, but let's put it out."

My brothers nodded in agreement and kicked gravel over the flames until they went out. This took a while. But when it was done, Mom was very relieved, until one of my brothers said, "Wait, that's not the cool part. This is the cool part."

He proceeded to show Mom the "cool part" as he kicked some of the gravel off, and the flames quickly burst back up with renewed vigor.

The result was a burned down fence and a charred power pole. Turns out, Napalm is really hard to extinguish.

\* \* \*

Mom once walked outside looking for the boys, when she spotted them and some friends out in the hayfield playing. The playing came to an abrupt end when Mom noticed what this new game was.

It was known as Robin Hood Chicken. All the "players" stood in a tight circle around the one player in the middle, who had a bow and arrow. The arrow would be shot straight up into the sky, and the first one to bolt from the circle as the arrow returned to earth was, well, chicken.

There were close calls, and though no one ever got hurt, she forbid us from playing that game.

So we made sure she never caught us again …

\* \* \*

Our family *used* to be invited to wild-game dinners where everyone would bring something from the previous hunting season. Most everyone would bring the standard venison or pheasant dish, but Dad thought more unique recipes should be tried, so we always brought something like porcupine, beaver, raccoon, or muskrat.

That year, Dad decided to cook up some rattlesnake. Since we caught and skinned rattlesnakes constantly, he decided to prepare one for a meal. He caught one, beheaded it, skinned, and gutted it. He put it in a bowl of saltwater to marinate overnight. Sadly, he did not take in the fact that snakes, due to their high level of independent nerve functions and slow metabolism, can indeed move for quite a while after death.

This came as quite a shock to my mother when she opened the fridge up in the morning to find this headless, skinned snake of only muscle and skeleton wrapped around the condiments in the door and—to hear her tell it—still moving.

Now no one could place any animal in the fridge; Dad ruined it for us all.

\* \* \*

My frugal father decided he was tired of buying small vials of maggots for ice-fishing bait, so he decided to order in bulk. Where did he keep these you might ask? ... The house fridge, of course.

You need to keep them cold to stop them from pupating into flies. Apparently, he didn't think maggots met the "any animal" criteria, most likely since they fell into the insect genus. Leave it to a biologist to find a loophole. The crisper drawer was just the right temp and humidity, and worked great until, one time, the lid on the container was not properly re-sealed.

The next day, my mother pulled out a head of lettuce for BLTs. She slammed the head of lettuce on the counter to decore it, where promptly, a thousand maggots that had climbed in between the cool leaves of the lettuce flew everywhere across the counter in a grotesque maggoty explosion. They went across the floor and in large arcs across the room.

We had a lot of flies in the house that week, and my father had to get an outdoor fridge.

\* \* \*

My aunt Susan bought one of those hand-crank meat grinders for my mother, which she was quite happy with, until one day when she couldn't find it. She left the house and found my father in the garage with his back to her, working feverishly on an unknown project.

She spoke and apparently startled him, since he turned around quickly. Once his body was no longer between her and his project, she could see her meat grinder on the workbench behind him with the tail of a mouse still protruding from the top.

(Dad used to pay us five cents for every mouse we caught and brought him. I didn't know what happened to them afterward until this story was told.)

Dad wanted to make his own coyote lure. That meat grinder stayed in the garage after that. Dad's defense was that she never used it anyway, and his new lure concoction, which he named "Mickey," worked very well that trapping season.

\* \* \*

My mother is famous for reading in the bathroom. Once upon a time, my mother was sitting in the bathroom very late at night and bored. She forgot her book. She heard a strange sound like somebody in the house, then realized it was just the furnace kicking on.

That got her thinking. It is probably a thought many women have had: "Could my husband hear me and come to my rescue if I needed him?"

This is slightly more relevant to my family because my father was born deaf in one ear, and most of his hearing in the other had been compromised by early experiences with construction work and unprotected but judicial use of firearms. He tends to sleep upon his semigood ear and slumbers like a rock, quite successfully I might add.

The bathroom happens to share a wall with the bedroom. So experimentally, Mom decides to call out, "Help," in a conversational voice, or so it started. Upon this failing and eliciting no response from the hibernating mountain man, her voice grew in volume exponentially, increasing after each failed attempt.

Still no response from the sleeping husband.

Now my mother is getting mad. "I could get killed and he would dream through it," She said to herself.

Unknown to my mother, at this very moment, my father heard a very muffled "Humph," so he rolled off his good ear just in time to receive the next full-blown blast from my mother. You know the one, the level ten, veins popping out of the neck, blood-curdling death cry.

The wife at this point hears her once peaceful, slumbering, snoring husband bounce out of bed against the wall, slam into the door, off the door jamb, and down the hallway like a drunken pinball, straight toward the bathroom.

*Bam!* The bathroom door flies open.

My mother is still sitting peacefully in the bathroom while the hyperventilating husband pants and searches the room with wild eyes.

"What's wrong? What's wrong?" my father yells while still seeking the source of danger.

My unabashed mother replies quietly while feeling bad about the whole thing, "Oh, nothing honey. Just seeing if you could hear me if I needed you to."

My mother didn't test out my father's hearing anymore after that, and Dad got to replace a broken bathroom door.

# Ten-Gallon Hat

A cowboy walks into a bar and sits down. The bartender comes over and asks him what he wants to drink. He takes off his ten-gallon hat, and lo and behold, a toad is growing right out of the top of his head.

In astonishment, the bartender asks, "What in the world happened to you?"

The toad replied, "I don't know, it started out as a wart on my butt."

# Boy Gone Fishing

It's the time of year, and branding season has come: the time to burn a brand on the calves as well as tag and administer medication, and so forth.

We lived on the Overcast's ranch. They were our neighbor's, landlords, and our adopted second family.

The homestead is a mess of activity since this is all happening right outside our house, and my whole family was pitching in. Branding is not a quiet affair. It's kind of like a jet engine made of animals, a constant hum and roar.

No one was letting me help with the branding on account of me being four. I still hadn't proven myself, you see.

*How is a four-year-old supposed to prove himself if they never let me in the ring with the beasts?* I had tried sneaking my way into the fray, bringing snacks, and trying to look busy so I could stick around. Somehow, they saw through that ploy and sent me packing each time.

So … I went looking for something else to do. I had already taken my daily bombing run in my B-17 Flying Fortress, also known as the tree out back, in which I had installed a cockpit of sorts. It had to be refueled anyway.

There was always the sandbox, but after that last ambush blindsided me and left most of my platoon buried, I couldn't force myself to go back to that slaughter. Plus, I didn't want to spend time finding all the buried plastic army men.

I couldn't go play in Fort Rope out in the trees, on account of there being a lot of newly branded and ticked off cows and calves residing in that area. *What's a kid to do?*

I decided I was going fishing. I grabbed my rod, some basic tackle, and I was off.

My brothers had made a small raft out of two fifty-five-gallon drums and whatever wood they could get off of Dad. It was held together by miles of orange baling twine (most likely stolen from the Overcasts) with sturdy, experimental Boy Scout knots. It didn't look very seaworthy, mind you, but I figured I could make it work for a little trout run.

I was not allowed to venture down to the creek without a big person with me. I had taken a few trips with my brothers when the water was lower. Since they were busy branding, and I was much older since the directive had been given—it had to have been at least two weeks—I made an executive decision: I would skipper it myself. I felt like Huck Finn on his first adventure.

Though my family says otherwise, I remember what happened next vividly.

The little creek that runs through our yard is flooding. Needless to say, the creek is not very small anymore.

I had never seen the water this high. Our normally quiet stream was now a river. Cold, black roiling water, with debris and junk picked up along its route, going as fast as a speeding car.

I was glad to see the conditions for this voyage were favorable.

Just another challenge to be overcome by Skipper Tim. However, thinking back, if the skipper had remembered he didn't know how to swim yet, he might have done some things differently.

The trusty raft was still tied to our makeshift dock, which was made up of more stolen lumber and twine. The dock was now submerged, with the raft fighting the tether. Another warning sign, it would seem, but one I quickly disregarded as I tossed my tackle onto the raft and placed one foot upon it.

That's where the trouble started. The raft, being a raft, moved.

Now I'm doing the splits but maintaining balance, like a ninja I might add, for about twenty minutes. I fought the forces of gravity while trying to pull the raft back to the shore. My legs were shaking at this point, and I decided it was time for some big people's help. I started yelling. While it was fairly quiet down near the creek, I forgot that up top, it was still an animal jet engine. I kept yelling.

Around this time, my mom is up top supervising the work, the branding is going well, everyone seems to know their jobs, and the whole thing is progressing quite nicely. A random thought shoots across her mind, *Where's Tim?* She sees one of the older laborers walk by (also known as one of her sons), and calls out, "Have you seen Tim?"

"I think I saw him walking down to the stream about five minutes ago with a fishing pole," the laborer says.

Mom decides to investigate since, only about a week ago, she caught the little rapscallion sitting on the peak of the house. *I still do not know how he even got up there*, she thinks as she starts walking down to the stream.

My legs are shaking. I look down, black water is rushing by, frothing. Now I remember the thing about not being able to swim. Lovely! Finally, the waterlogged grass gives way on my left foot. With one final, earth-shattering yell, I plunge into the murky depths.

While walking down to the stream, my mother thinks she hears a little "Heeeeellllpppp." She decides to grab some of the laborers and head down to the stream at a slight jog.

The water rushes over me. It's so cold I lose my breath. I rise to the surface grabbing a breath of air. The current is dragging me downstream. I grab … nothing. I grab again … still nothing. I go under again. I come up again, another breath. I grab … Yes, grass! I get one hand on the grass clump. I try to get a foot up, but the whole stream is deeply undercut by the rushing water, nothing to get a foot on.

Five minutes go by, then ten. The grass pulls out. Back under I go. Another clump of grass, I grab on with both hands desperately. I'm *not* going back under! I hold out with incredible stamina and strength. Water splashing over my face, grabbing a breath of air here and there, another ten minutes goes by. I start yelling with what little air I have left. I give it all I've got.

Mom and a few of the laborers get down to the dock. The raft is still bobbing back and forth, supporting only a lonely tackle box. They hear a little "ahugggughhgaaaeellp" coming from downstream a little way.

I've given it all I got, arms straining, shaking, so cold … can't breathe. *It seems to be getting dark; the sun must be setting. I started this around noon, right?* As I'm about to lose my grip, big people hands grab me by the arms and pull me up.

My mom says I was holding on to the grass, eyes big as saucers, as they pulled me out.

My dad says my hair wasn't even wet.

Whatever happened, the little master and commander lived to fight another day and … had to start swimming lessons.

# Yogi-ism

"The future ain't what it used to be."

# Pieces Is Pieces and Parts Is Parts, or Anything for a Buck

My dad holds to the principle that any hobby should pay for itself. That meant if you went hunting or fishing, you better come back with meat. It also meant that to pay for gas and supplies, you better pick up anything along the way that had any value. Dad learned that there was a market for almost anything.

That meant that you kept your eyes open for shed antlers, owl pellets (look it up), and any salvageable fur that was found lying on the highway. Dad would always whip around on the highway to pick up a road-killed fox, badger, or raccoon because, as he explained, "We better get it before somebody else does." I mean everybody is out after roadkill, right?

One time, we pulled over on a narrow state highway to retrieve a raccoon. Dad told my brother in the back seat that he would just drive up alongside it, and to "real quick" just grab him and throw him in, as to not block traffic.

When my brother reached down to grab him he said, "But, Dad, he's still alive."

Not to be thwarted, Dad told him to just take the .22 rifle in the back, stick it out the open door and shoot him. As he started to get the gun, Dad happened to look up to see a Highway Patrol parked opposite us on the highway.

He hollered at my brother to stop, opened his window to hear the officer say, "Everything okay? You need help?"

Dad told him, "We're good, we're good," and off we went.

I know it bothered Dad terribly to lose that critter even though he could have had his mug shot on the wall at the post office.

* * *

Collecting and selling skunk essence was another side project. Yes, there is a market for almost anything.

Skunks were plentiful on the trap line, and Dad would kill them with a euthanasia solution injected through a syringe on a long pole so they wouldn't spray. Then he would take another syringe and withdraw the essence from their glands and store it in pop bottles. He would cap, tape, and wax the bottles to contain the smell, wrap them in foam and plastic and ship it to a dealer.

Despite all these efforts, the project came to a screeching halt when our UPS man said he could no longer ship it because some of his clients were complaining that their Christmas gifts smelled funny.

What a bunch of grinches!

* * *

One thing we never passed up was a porcupine. The long hairs on a porcupine's back—not the quills—were bringing premium prices.

After a long day of deer hunting, my dad and brother were coming down a mountain road when Dad spotted a porcupine in a tree a hundred yards off the road. Dad got out his rifle, got a steady aim, shot, and plunked him. The porcupine never moved, but Dad knew he had hit him, so he went over to wait for him to fall.

My brother Kody decided to go wait in the truck, because it was bitterly cold, and instantly fell asleep.

When Dad got there, he realized that someone else had already shot the porcupine, and it was locked in a death grip on the tree. It had been there a while, because it had started to rot, and a pile of quills had fallen out on the ground below it. Not to be denied this prize, he shook the tree for quite a while to dislodge it. It just wouldn't move, so he devised a plan.

It was about fifteen feet up in the, air and there was a straight, skinny poplar bending out close enough to it that he thought he could shimmy up and unhook it. Just like firemen climb trees to rescue kittens. My Dad is kinda like that, but he only does it for dead animals. Basically the same thing, right?

My dad crawled up the poplar next to it, and as planned, it bent perfectly toward the porcupine. He was able to reach over and unhook most of its claws from the branch. He was almost there when heard a loud *Snap!* The poplar broke at the base, pitching him straight down to the frozen hard ground.

From fifteen feet, he hit flat on his back. He said it knocked his wind out, and he felt like every bone was broken and every joint disjointed. He couldn't move for quite a while, and it took forever to get his breath back. As he started to regain awareness, he realized he had additional pains in his back, remember that before- mentioned quill pile? Yep, to add insult to multiple injuries, he'd landed right on it.

He started calling for Kody to help him out … to no avail. Kody was fast asleep.

Staring straight up in the sky, still immobile, he suddenly came to the realization that the object of his desire was hanging on by one precarious claw, swinging back and forth in the breeze like a pendulum of spikey death directly above him.

The potential aspect of the quill pig landing on his face made his current aches and pains seem not so important. With everything he had, he crawled and eventually hobbled to the truck. He plopped behind the steering wheel in a contorted fashion and headed home. All the way home he kept having my brother reach behind his back and pull quills out.

Things don't always work out in life, but if you're passionate about your hobbies, you'll do anything for a buck. Even if you fall from a tree into a pile of quills, pieces is still pieces and parts is parts.

# Frog Loan

A frog hops into a bank and jumps up on the teller's window.

"Can I help you?" the teller asks.

"I'm here to get a loan," the frog replies.

"Well, you'll have to see our loan officer, Patty Black," the teller says.

So he hops over to her desk and says, "Are you, Patty Black? I'm here to get a loan."

"Yes, I am," she says. "What do you have for collateral?"

The frog pulls a tiny sack off his shoulder and opens it up.

She looks at it for a moment and then says, "I'll have to go talk to the bank president."

She goes into the bank president's office and says, "Sir, there's a frog out there who wants a loan, and when I asked him for collateral, he showed me this. I'm not sure what it is."

The bank president looks it over and says, "It's a knickknack, Patty Black, give the frog a loan."

CAUSE EFFECT

# Cause and Effect

My dad told us kids that we were all inflicted with a genetic disorder that came from Mom's side of the family. He told us It had to do with a nonfunctioning gene that he called the C&E gene, commonly known as the cause-and-effect gene.

As I have grown, I have reason to doubt his claim about Mom's side, as I think my father's blood is mentioned almost as much as all of us kids in these stories, and Mom was normally the one that had to clean up the scorch marks, scrub skunk essence, and all too often, act as a combat medic.

However, this anomaly was observable. It was best demonstrated by watching my older brothers.

The following series of events all started with Kirby falling off a second-story balcony at my grandpa's house onto the lawn. He missed the concrete patio below by inches.

That same afternoon, they were waiting on the dock for a tour ferryboat when Kirby decided to play down near the shore by the rocks. He happened to find a really cool, broken bottle and felt it needed to be broken a little bit more. In the process, he slashed his hand rather severely, which we wrapped up temporarily until my parents could get him to someone that could provide stitches, and then we boarded the ferryboat.

Dad, in desperate need of a break, handed out some lifesaver hard candy to all of the kids to keep them quiet so they could at least enjoy the boat ride, but soon, Mom noticed Kirby was shivering and turning blue. After a few Heimlich maneuvers, he regained his color. If not for the small hole in the aptly named candy, he might have passed out.

* * *

On a separate family trip not long after the previously mentioned series of unfortunate events, the family went fishing for northern pike. Dad showed the boys how to hold a northern pike tightly over the gills to remove the hooks. Kirby landed a good-size pike, and in the process of removing the lure, he let up on his grip, and the fish twisted and drove two treble hooks into the palm of his freshly healed hand he had just had the stitches removed from.

The fish was flopping around the bottom of the boat with my brother attached. Since the fish was about half of Kirby's body weight at the time, it was tossing him around. Kirby handled it as good as anyone would, I think. Which is to say, not very well.

Finally pinning the fish down, Dad got some pliers and pinched the barbs down so he could extricate the hooks.

More blood.

When asked why he didn't just cut off the barbs, Dad replied that he didn't want to ruin the lure.

Upon returning to shore and saving his valuable lure from my brother's hand, Dad got the great idea that Mom should get out of camp and go on a boat ride with him. Mom argued that the boys couldn't be left at camp alone, but after a while, he persuaded her that it would only be a half hour, saying, "What could possibly go wrong in that time?"

(Now that I'm older, I'm thinking there might have been some hanky-panky involved in my parents' little trip).

The boys were told, "Do not do anything while we are gone."

When Mom and Dad returned to camp, they found blood all around the camper and my brothers tucked into their sleeping bags, peeking out with apprehension. (Nothing suspicious about three boys quietly tucked into their beds in the middle of the afternoon, right?) Jesse had his arm all bandaged up in gauze. The story came out that they were bored and decided to cut a little kindling for the fire.

Being pretty small and not able to lift the ax, they devised a plan in which Jesse would sink a hatchet into a log and hold on to it while Kirby took a hammer and pounded it down through. This worked pretty well until a glancing blow from the hammer chipped a sharp metal shard off of the hatchet and buried it in Jesse's forearm. That alone was pretty shocking, but when he pulled it out, it apparently had driven directly into an artery, and blood started squirting all over. Fortunately, we had made friends with the people in an RV next door to our camp, and she happened to be a nurse with a complete medical kit.

Mom ripped Dad a new one: "What could poss-abily go wrong in that amount of time?"

The next day, they were breaking camp. They had a broken fishing pole from the previous day that Dad told Kirby to throw in the dumpster. As he was getting ready to throw it in, he somehow surmised that it should be broken again before discarding it. So he broke it over his knee. The only problem was that it broke at the guide, which his hand was on, and the sharp metal base drove completely through two fingers and pinned them together.

He came walking back to camp with a short piece of the fishing pole attached to his hand.

More blood.

And now, with both of his hands in bandages, I think we owe those campers next to us for first-aid supplies. Too bad it wasn't closer to Halloween. He would have made a convincing mummy.

*   *   *

The folks were glad to get us back home without any mortalities, and our normal routines resumed. At this point in his life, Kirby had been cultivating a massive curly afro-like hairdo that he was quite proud of.

One of Kirby's chores was to take the garbage out to the burn barrel. For those of you who don't live in the country, the burn barrel is a fifty-five-gallon drum in which any burnable garbage gets dumped and eventually burned. The only hard rule is that you have to presort the garbage and remove any aerosol cans. The rule was apparently overlooked this time when my brother lit the barrel and began playing in the backyard.

Dad had just exited the house when—*Boom!*—an aerosol can blew up in the burn barrel. Kirby's eyes got big, and then he looked over at Dad and sheepishly began walking toward him to get a chewing out.

As he was walking across the yard, a whistling sound was heard coming from the sky. Before he got to Dad, a flaming ball of melted plastic milk jug landed squarely on the top of his head.

The burn barrel had acted as a mortar tube, the aerosol can the propellant, and an empty milk jug the ordinance. Dad quickly got to him and beat him on the head to put the fire out. (I think he secretly enjoyed that for several reasons). That was the end of Kirby's illustrious hairdo.

While Kirby was taken to the hospital, there are two versions of how he got there. Knowing my father's sense of humor, I'm inclined to believe my brother's version of the story, which has my Mom driving to the hospital with Dad and the smoldering brother in the back seat, because my Dad was unable to drive due to uncontrollably laughing.

\* \* \*

These episodes have afflicted us our whole lives, and these are only a few of many more. This gene problem is with us forever, as age apparently makes no difference, and there is no known cure. We just make sure we have a fully stocked medical kit handy.

# Peg-Leg Pig

A county extension agent was visiting with a farmer
when he noticed a pig walk by with a peg leg. Intrigued,
he asked the farmer, "What's with the peg leg?"

The farmer replied, "Let me tell you about that special pig. One day,
I was plowing over on the south forty when my tractor tipped over
and pinned me to the ground. That pig saw me out there and ran
over and dug me out from underneath that thing—saved my life."

The agent said, "Wow, that is special. But what about the peg leg?"

"That's not all of it," the farmer added. "Another time, our house caught
on fire during the night, and that pig smelled the smoke, came to our
bedroom window and saved me and the wife. That is one special pig."

The agent replied, "But what about the peg-
leg. Did he burn his leg in the fire?"

The farmer replied, "No, not really. But when you've got a
special pig like that, you don't eat him all at one time."

Illustration by Dave McGee 2020

# Pistol-Packin' Prolapse

When my folks relocated to a little town in North Central Montana called Chinook, they met a nice couple, Ken (Kenny) and Dawn Overcast, who invited them to rent a vacant farmhouse directly across the creek from their place. We grew up with their kids on the ranch, and they became more like family than friends.

When we first moved there, Dad told Kenny and Dawn to give him a call if they ever needed help on the ranch. You have to understand that Dad wasn't too far removed from Chicago at the moment and had spent all his time in Montana so far developing his fishing, hunting, and trapping skills. He had never taken the time to learn much about ranching and farming, and certainly had not learned the associated lingo.

Hence follows the next story, which happened in the early 1990s and is best told by my father Kent Gilge.

\* \* \*

One thing you have to understand about Dawn is that although she's this sweet, five-foot-nothing woman, when she is on a mission and starts barking orders, *everybody* jumps.

It was spring, and Kenny was off on business for a few days and had left the calving duties to Dawn. About one o'clock in the morning, I was rousted from a deep sleep by a phone call. It was Dawn. In her military-like voice, she said, "I got a prolapse in the calving shed, I need you right now … click."

*A pro-lapse*, I said to myself. I'd been taking care of raccoon/skunk problems in the neighborhood, but this was a new one. *What kind of critter is a prolapse?* In my defense, I was quite groggy. All I could think of was, *Should I take the shotgun or the pistol?* I settled on the pistol, threw on some clothes, and headed across the creek.

I noticed a faint light at the back of the corral, and as I approached, I heard some voices. I found Dawn and a family friend, Gary, standing over a cow lying on the straw that had just given birth. The cow had expelled its uterus, which was lying out behind her. I put my pistol in my coat pocket and stood there dumbfounded. Dawn and Gary were discussing the next move and rummaging around in a Band-Aid can for sutures with a flashlight that put off a dull glow.

I think the batteries in that flashlight had last been replaced in about 1962. They then explained the plan to me. My job was to lay down behind the cow, place my fist in the center of the uterus, push it back in as far as I could, and hold it there while Gary sewed everything up to hold it in place. I shed my coat, assumed my position, and reinserted the uterus. That's when the battle began. I was fully stretched out on the straw with my arm in up to the elbow when the contractions began. The contractions pushed my entire body back against the shed wall. I set my feet against the wall and pushed back. The contractions were so strong they were crushing my forearm and I soon lost blood circulation.

Meanwhile, Dawn and Gary are arguing about what needle and thread to use. I expressed in what I like to think was a calm, professional tone a deep and sincere desire for them to hurry up, as this cow's insides wanted to be on the outside really bad, and I didn't know how long I could do this.

It felt like my arm was in an industrial car crusher. The contractions were coming about every forty-five seconds, and I realized I had to switch arms. Any letup at all, and the uterus would be expelled again, so between contractions, I slipped my left arm in alongside my right arm, in an effort to extricate my crushed right arm.

Just as I slipped my left arm in, I was hit with another contraction that pinned both arms inside like handcuffs. My elbows were touching. As the contraction let up, I was able to remove my limp right arm, and Gary began sewing. It seemed like it took forever, and I began to wonder, *If Gary slips, will I be permanently attached to this cow?* This was entirely a possibility, as I had no feeling in my arm.

I was finally able to extricate myself, said good night, and headed for the shower. I had about a half a bale of straw glued to me with manure and afterbirth.

Any aspirations I had of becoming a cowboy were gone. I woke up the next morning with bruised arms and a whole new appreciation for childbirth.

\* \* \*

This is just one story/adventure of many that the Gilges and Overcasts would share, not the greatest nor the least. We lived there a long time but finally had to leave after we had a fish fry get out of control, and we burned the house down.

Dad was gone at the time, and the boys were able to salvage the guns and the photographs before the house was engulfed in flames. Dad said it was then that he realized for the first time he had raised us boy's right.

We heard from others later that Kenny was telling people, "I had this family living across the creek that I'd been trying, without success, to get rid of for a long time, and I finally had to burn 'em out."

# Yogi-ism

"No one goes there anymore. It's too crowded."

# Rest-Stop Etiquette, and First Impressions

by Kent Gilge

The wife and I were returning from Chicago back home to Montana when the coffee caught up with me, and I pulled into a rest area in North Dakota. It had been a long stint behind the wheel. It was late, getting dark, and I was really groggy. I needed to stretch and wake up as much as anything.

There isn't much that impresses me about North Dakota except its rest areas. This one was brand-new and space-age. As I walked into the men's room I was impressed with everything. All the fixtures, including the mirrors, were of polished stainless steel and designed like something from NASA.

A guy was standing at one urinal, and I sauntered up to the one next to him. I noticed him glance over at me a few times, which creeped me out a little bit. When he finished, I watched him, in the mirror, slowly exit, looking over his shoulder at me with kind of a bewildered/astonished look on his face. Then it hit me. Why is there a mirror over my urinal?

I finished and stepped back. That's when I noticed the urinal I had, was different than the one he had. Well actually, the sink I was peeing in had no faucets, as it was one of those motion-activated ones that just spray water out of a hole, and it was apparently low to the ground so kids could use it.

I killed some time inside the restroom, hoping this guy had left, but when I exited, I could see him sitting in his car with his wife, pointing me out.

I guess the only thing I could have done worse is if I'd gone number two or ended up in the women's restroom.

\* \* \*

Driving stories are always good, especially in Montana. Its normal to drive one to two hundred miles if you want to visit another town, sometimes without even seeing another person or vehicle. This is expressed well by my father (Tim's now late grandpa) in the next story.

\* \* \*

My mom and dad were planning to drive out from their home in Chicago to Montana for the first time, and I couldn't wait to show my dad what Montana had to offer. I'd told him for years about all the hunting opportunities and wild game Montana was famous for. I tried to explain to him about the incredible wide-open spaces and why they call it the Big Sky Country. I was going to take him hunting and show him what a wildlife mecca we had here.

When they arrived, Dad started talking about all the dead wildlife on the road. I thought he was concurring with me about our abundant wildlife, but then he added, "Your animals out here must be suicidal."

I looked quizzically at him, and he continued. "Every mile, there was a road-killed critter, but I drove for half an hour at a time without seeing another vehicle. They must just wait by the roadside and jump out in front of a car when they see one. For God's sake, I've seen a squirrel successfully cross eight lanes of rush-hour traffic on the Eisenhower Expressway!"

So much for first impressions.

# One Wish

A man was walking along the beach in California when he came upon a bottle. He picked it up and played with it a little and out came a genie.

The genie said, "Well, you let me out, so you get one wish."

The man thought a little bit and said, "I've always wanted to go to Hawaii, but I'm afraid to fly, and I get seasick on boats. So I'd like you to build me a bridge from here to Hawaii so I can drive over there."

The genie got very agitated and said, "Do you have any idea what kind of an engineering feat that would be? Isn't there anything you would rather have?"

The man replied, "Well, perhaps you could explain to me the mind of a woman?

The genie replied, "Would you like that highway to be a two-lane or a four-lane."

# Shortcuts Are Hard

*It's supposed to be a challenge, that's why they call it a short-cut. If it was easy, it would just be the way.*
— Rubin from *Road Trip*

My brothers Jesse and Kody went to live in Hawaii in their early twenties. At this point, it's unclear how long they planned to stay, but by using one-way tickets and showing up with very little money (the equivalent of

Cortés burning the boats), it's obvious they planned to stay awhile. This plan changed at some point in the next few months when they realized mainlanders were not highly regarded there. They were haoles, white foreigners, and generally treated very poorly by the locals.

Work was hard to find, and eating a couple of cans of tuna a day was getting old. They managed to scrape some funds together to get tickets home after four months, but that is a whole other story we'll save for another time.

They lived on the big island, and about a week before their flight home, they decided they wanted one more adventure. They had never been to a waterfall in the heart of Hawaii called Hiilawe in the Waipio Valley.

Some friends they had met touted that there was a thousand-foot waterfall. They had never seen it but knew where the trail was that supposedly lead to it, so they left first thing in the morning. The entrance to the hike was through a field, and it was not a tourist spot, most likely because the hike was so long and grueling.

While walking up, they passed what looked like man-made, carved aqueducts, sometimes carved directly into the stone, sometimes made with walls of stones. They asked their friends/guides about them and were told that they were made by the Pygmies. The Pygmies are a mythological dwarf also known as the Menehune, which were known for building massive and incredible structures overnight. Jesse and Kody's friends said that there were many such waterways all over the islands.

After about half the day was past, and many miles of hiking and a couple of thousand feet of elevation gained, they arrived. The waterfall was across a giant ravine and dropped over 1,400 feet. They stood and took in this amazing sight. The waterfall pouring down through the clouds and continuing out of sight below was breathtaking.

After an hour of admiring the site, the group decided to head back down the mountain so they could be home before dark. My brothers noticed another Menehune trench just down from where they stood. It looked like the same trench they saw at the bottom of the mountain, and they had a thought.

They could either hike the five hours back down, or they could just slide down the mountain and stay cool while doing it. Seemed like a good shortcut and a no-brainer—let gravity do the work.

The friends thought otherwise and headed back down on foot. After each throwing in a good-luck chew from their only Copenhagen can, Jesse and Kody stepped into the waterslide-like ditch and proceeded to coast comfortably down the mountain. This ditch didn't follow the hiking trail; it split off on its own path into the mountains, but in the same general direction, so the plan felt solid.

After about half a mile, the plan hit a snag. The trench went straight into a hole in the side of a mountain. They slowed their slide and stopped before the entrance, which was about four feet tall and looked to be man-made as well. Looking through the hole, they could see some daylight. It was small but it was light. The question was, If they could see light, could it be anything other than the tunnel coming out the other side? After some discussion, they decided it only made sense that the little glimpse of light must be the exit to their waterslide, and the decision was made.

They pulled up their feet, and in they went. The water wasn't going that fast, so it didn't feel reckless. But after what seemed like an eternity, the little light at the end of the tunnel didn't seem to be changing at all.

At one point, Kody yelled to Jesse, "I don't think that light is getting any bigger!"

Nothing to do now but keep going, there was no way to turn around.

The deeper they went, the faster the water went. Only their heads were above the water, with the ceiling of the tunnel about a foot above that. However, they could not see the stalactites hanging from the ceiling until they found them with their faces and tops of their head. With the speed they were now traveling, it was not a pleasant experience.

Suddenly, the light started to get bigger very quickly, and they heard the sound at the same time. Seeing that blessed exit hole meant they were saved from being trapped in an underground aquifer and drowning, but the sound—the sound was a roar of epic proportions that could only really be one thing: a waterfall.

The light was approaching too fast, and they had no idea what was on the other side of it. Desperately they grasped, dragged, and pulled on anything they could to slow themselves, pushing onto the walls and grinding their hands against the stone. By God's grace, they were able to stop about fifteen feet short of the opening and slowly work their way toward the exit it to take a peek …

The water was pushing against them pretty hard, so they had to stay close to the side of the tunnel and hold on to the rocks while they stuck their heads out to see what awaited them. What they saw was not good. Water shot out and down, clashed with a giant rock pile about seventy feet below them, and then past that to rocks at the bottom of the canyon another 150 feet below. Grasping onto the sides of the tunnel for dear life as water dragged at their clothes, trying to pull them out, they slipped out of the tunnel and stood on small rock ledges right next to the exit.

In Hawaii, much of the volcanic rock is covered with thick, spongelike moss, up to several feet thick at times. This same spongelike surface covered the side of the mountain they had found themselves on. Kody had the idea to punch their arms into it, all the way to the armpits. After a sketchy check on the strength of it, it appeared as though with their arms sunk in all the way, it would support their entire weight. Kody led the way, slowly zigzagging his way down the cliff wall next to the waterfall, and Jesse followed, using the same arm and foot holes created by Kody.

After a long time, they reached the bottom, with adrenaline rushing and arms feeling like jelly. At one point, one or the other brothers mentions that this may not be the shortcut they thought it was.

Free from the threat of imminent death for the moment, they took stock and tried to figure out what was next. They were now deep down in the narrow canyon floor, with mountains shooting almost straight up on either side of them, thousands of feet.

It made the decision easy, there was no way but down. They decided the throw in another chew, as it seemed to help their fate up to this point, but somewhere in the tunnel or climb down, the can of Copenhagen had been lost. Despair nearly took them then.

With downtrodden hearts, they moved on without it. Fortunately, it looked as though the original plan was still intact, as the waterslide-like aqueduct continued out of the pool from the waterfall, so on they went. This was short-lived, however, as the ditch disappeared. They were now wading/floating down a rocky stream. The warm Caribbean feel of Hawaii was gone as well. High in the shaded canyons of the mountains the temperature had dropped into the low fifties. Not enough to freeze you solid, but spend a few hours soaking wet with nothing on but shorts in fifty-degree weather is not comfortable, to say the least.

After another half-mile, they got to another drop-off, this one a sixty-foot waterfall. Not being able to see how deep the water was at the bottom, jumping was not ideal. Fortunately, the walls around them and down the cliffs to the pool was the same spongelike surface that saved them from the tunnel. While contemplating the plan, they got a huge boost. Their life-saving can of

Copenhagen bounced off Kody's leg, and he was able to grab it. It was a little waterlogged, but that didn't matter right then. It was the lift they needed.

They packed a soggy lip full of the soft chew, and with renewed energy, they continued. They employed the same strategy as before. This time with Jesse leading the way. The climb down had to follow the moss, which led away from the waterfall about forty feet before continuing down. After making it out to this spot and then down ten feet to where a small shrub-like tree grew out of the side of the cliff, Jesse looked back to see where Kody was. Kody was using the same holes and was making his way out. Everything looked good … That lasted about five more seconds.

When Kody was fifteen feet away from the spot to start working down to Jesse, the moss fell away under Kody. A twenty-by-twenty-foot section detached from the cliff and fell some fifty feet to the rocks below. Fortunately, the weak point in the moss started at Kody's midsection, so with his arms deep in the moss above, Kody's lower body hung in free space with his arms holding him from following the moss to the bottom.

After a brief discussion, Jesse was able to stomp a small platform in the moss at the base of the tree. Hoping it was stable enough for a landing, Kody swung himself side to side to create momentum. After a few swings, Kody pulled his arms from the wall, launching toward the platform.

Kody's ninja-warrior-type skills paid off, and he landed on the platform, grabbing at the tree and Jesse, as Jesse kept one arm deep in the moss in hope of being an anchor. Everything came to a stop, and they were both still there, grasping the wall and standing on the little two-foot platform.

After a few deep breaths, they made their way down to the bottom of the waterfall. They washed off in the pool and got ready to continue.

The outcome was not looking as bright, they were getting deeper and deeper in this canyon with no end in sight.

As they continued down the stream, the terrain remained the same, with one exception, the once moss-covered walls next to them changed into flat, vertical sheer rock. Hopefully, they wouldn't have to do any more climbing down. That wishful thinking ended a few minutes later, as they found themselves on the top of another fifty-foot waterfall. After a while looking over the edge, Kody sees their Copenhagen can float by Jesse without him noticing and Kody lunged for the can, but it was out of reach, and it fell over the waterfall. It must have fallen out of a pocket during the cliff wall jump.

They decided this was an omen and a sign, if "the can" (as it was now referred to) could make the jump, so could they. I personally think they just really wanted that Copenhagen. They both made the jump without knowing the depth of the water (which is very, very stupid).

Had it been only a few feet deep, the journey and this story would have ended abruptly right there. Yet with another stroke of luck, or the hand of God on their lives, the water was deep.

Upon emerging from the jump, they failed to find the Copenhagen, a demoralizing blow. They had no choice but to continue without it. After another hour in the stream and five hours total into this descent, the sun was setting, and the temperature continued to drop. They were cut up, shaking from exhaustion, and shivering from the cold. I imagine the reality had to have fully set in that they had no idea where they were or where this stream was heading. They did know that anything down was good. On an island, *down* led to the ocean. If you can get to the ocean, you can find a road.

While it was highly unlikely to find a friendly driver to pick them up (based on the percentage of nice people they had met on the island so far), a road would get them to Kona. On top of that, the temperature down at the ocean never dropped below seventy, so they knew they wouldn't freeze to death. Without knowing where they were, the discussion shifted to lasting the night and making the final push down in the morning. They had to get out of this water and try to warm up a bit while looking for a spot to huddle up for the night.

And while this may seem too farfetched, both swear it to be true. There, floating by the bank of the stream, was—you guessed it—the can.

The terrain had opened a bit; they were no longer packed in by sheer cliffs on either side. With another boost of energy, they climbed out of the water and started working their way through the brush and trees. All joking around had stopped, the focus was on trying to find a way to warm up and a place to stop. After not more than a hundred yards or so, they broke through the brush to find themselves standing at the base of the trail where the day had started. Their friends were there too, apparently in a debate on how long to wait before calling in a rescue.

After a few hugs and high fives, they headed for the cars.

Looking back on it now, Jesse says, at times, he'll think about how many narrow misses there were. So many times where, if one thing was off, instead of a great story, it would have been lives ending much too soon. But at the time, he didn't really think about that. They had this all-encompassing confidence.

I confirmed with both brothers that, for them, when they were together, they felt literally unstoppable. And this time, they were.

# Yogi-ism

"You can observe a lot by just watching."

# Treehouse Takeover

When I was about ten and my sister Katie was about eight, I really wanted a treehouse, but we didn't really have any trees that were strong enough or healthy enough for it. My dad pitched the idea of a pole-style fort near a tree, and that worked for me. However, Dad said we had to make something for my sister Katie first, or she would be upset.

We (Dad) worked hard over weeks building a real—miniature play-house. This thing had insulation and drywall, paint, carpet, power, and lights. Complete with miniature solid woodstove, shelves, refrigerator, seats, dishes, working windows and doors, among many other features. Just about the nicest playhouse you have ever seen. My sister Katie really liked it.

Once it was fully finished, we finally started on my basic fort: four tall poles and two short stuck and tamped into the ground, two platforms, and a ladder leading to each one. A railing around the platforms and a kind of fireman pole. Most of this was made from different scrap, including an old basketball hoop backboard we had laying around, all of it a patchwork of colors and quite ugly and very basic. I do not think it took us more than two or three days to get it finished.

The very next day, I wake up and excitedly go out to have my first adventure in my fort—only to find that it had been completely taken over. Oven and refrigerator on the upper deck, shelves put up, throw rugs on my platforms, and many other abominations.

My sister had completely emptied her playhouse and was having tea in my fort!

I was outraged and went immediately to my mother for a resolution. My sister was quite upset that she couldn't have the tree fort. What baffles us to this day, and in my opinion is one of the greatest mysteries in my life, is how she got it all up two stories on steep ladders by herself without anyone noticing ...

It took Dad and me quite a bit of work to get everything down from there and back into her house. She was a bean pole, weighing about as much as a wet bag of flower. She didn't weigh more than the solid woodstove set did ...

While writing this story, I asked my sister if she would finally tell me how she did it (for the sake of the book of course), and she still refused. My theories over the years have ranged from drugs—not likely—to an elaborate system of pullies, but perhaps my sister is just tough as nails, and when she wants something, she doesn't hold back.

Perhaps we can all learn something from that: work so hard that it makes others question how you did it.

# Charging Elephant

How do you keep an elephant from charging?

You take away its credit card.

# Infamous Driving

Mom always provided the family with a lot of interesting driving stories. Almost every time she returned from a trip to town, there would be a new dent or scratch in the car, and she would have no idea how it got there.

She once returned home and parked in the driveway with the rear tire very flat … and on fire.

When asked why she didn't realize she had a flat, she just shrugged and said, "I kind of noticed something, but I wasn't too far from home, so I thought I'd get back home, where Kent could fix it."

We got a Chevy Suburban once, and when she returned after her first drive into town, she said, "I like this car. People get out of my way."

She seemed to have almost a daily habit of locking the keys in the car. Dad thought he would solve the problem by stashing spare keys all over the outside and the underside of the car, but we would still get calls to help her out. When we would tell her to just get the key out from under the license plate or the windshield wiper or the one wired under the bumper, she would mention that they were all gone. When asked where they were, she would tell us they were all in the ashtray inside the car because she used them all last week.

Dad would get frustrated on long trips when he asked her to drive a little bit so he could get a nap. Not five minutes after they'd switch places, Dad would be awakened by the rumble strips on the side of the road, and she would announce, "You have to stay awake and talk to me, or I'll fall asleep."

It's hard to give her directions, because she once told Dad that whichever way the car was pointed was "north."

One of our favorites was when Dad gave her directions to get back to a friend's house about forty miles away in Ronan, Montana.

He told her to turn off on Highway 93 where there's a large Coeur d'Alene sign from the interstate. All she remembered was something about the Coeur d'Alene sign, so she went for it and ended up about two hundred miles away, having gone across the entire state of Idaho. She began to realize her mistake when she saw a Washington state sign near Spokane, which is when she decided to call Dad for help. This was before the days of cell phones.

My brother Kody's comment to this was, "It's a good thing there's an ocean over there. That might have stopped her."

# Chicken Facts

Do you know why a chicken coop always has two doors?

Cause if it had four doors it would be a chicken sedan.

# The Teachable Moment
by Kent Gilge

was driving along with my eight-year-old son when, out of the blue, he asks, "Dad, what's a eunuch?"

Now, the wife is always getting on my case about not making the best of teachable moments. We also decided that we would be straightforward with our children about questions regarding sexuality, so I dove right in. I explained that a eunuch was a male who had been castrated and therefore was impotent and had no real sexual desire.

My son was looking straight ahead, sort of dumbfounded, so I did my best to explain those terms. I mentioned that eunuchs were used, back in the olden days, by kings to oversee their harems. That required another flustered explanation.

By now, I realized I was over my head in this thing and asked him, "Does that answer your question?"

He looked at me quizzically and said, "No, not really. I just wanted to know why ... on the cop shows ... they get on the radio and say, 'Attention, all eunuchs.'"

So much for the teachable moment.

# Yogi-ism

"Ninety percent of the game is half mental."

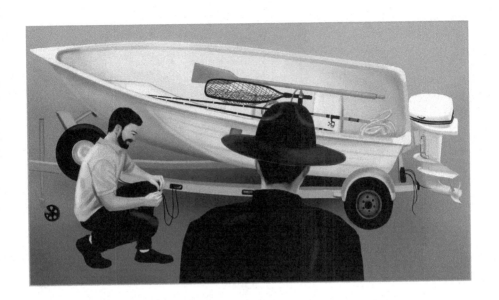

# By a Trailer's Dying Light

I n the spring, when Dad heard the walleye were biting, he grabbed Kody and drove out to the lake.

In his rush to get there, he'd hitched up the trailer in a hurry before hopping on Highway 15, his thoughts fully focused on the large number of fish they would catch. When he saw the flashing lights in his rearview, he wondered if he'd been speeding along this last leg of the road.

He was in a hurry not to miss the walleye bite, so he jumped out and headed toward the officer to see what was up. (Not something you should do with an officer, but in small towns back in the day, not something uncommon)

He met the officer at the back of the truck and said, "Man, was I speeding? I guess I got excited trying to get to the lake because I heard the walleye are biting."

The officer calmly explained that, no, he had a taillight issue on the boat trailer.

Being in a hurry, Dad started going on about how the lights worked the last time he was out and assured him it was probably a loose or corroded wire in the plug, which he vigorously started jockeying with. He hollered at Kody to pump the brakes.

The officer was back behind the boat by now. He looked up at the officer, who showed no sign that he had fixed the problem, so Dad went on to explain that the trailer was grounded through the ball and that it probably wasn't making a good connection.

Dad proceeded to reef back and forth on the tongue and hitch like the unanointed knights trying to get the sword out of the stone.

"Kody, pump the brakes again!"

Dad looked back at the silently still patrolman, who simply motioned him to the back of the boat trailer with his index finger. He followed to see what the officer was staring at, which was, in fact, virtually nothing. By that, I mean there were no taillights, bulbs, or even sockets, only a few wires dangling in the breeze.

It was then that Dad remembered, the week before, he had driven on a seventy-five-mile trip to another lake that was entirely on rough gravel roads, which had pummeled everything to smithereens. He then began a long apology and offered to return home, which wasn't far away, and repair them so he could get in on the walleye bite before it was over.

The patrolman could hardly keep from laughing and was apparently so impressed with the show and associated rhetoric that he told him to just go fishing and get home by dark. Most police officers in Montana are good hardworking Americans who can appreciate a good walleye bite.

The catch was great that day, but the story Kody told while reenacting Dad jumping around, hitting, and pulling on things when they got home that night was better.

# Thermos

Bob and Jim were visiting when Bob asked,
"What's that fancy jug you got there?"

"It's my new thermos bottle," Jim said.

"What does it do?" Bob asked.

"Well, the salesman said it keeps hot things hot
and cold things cold," Jim stated.

"No kidding. What you got in it?" Bob asked with real curiosity.

"Some coffee and a popsicle for later," Jim said enthusiastically.

Kenneth Gilge
Graduation

# "Life Is Hard. It's Harder when You're Stupid."

## —Grandpa Gilge

Mom and Dad would leave us alone for short periods for important things. We always had something preplanned and looked forward to those occasions. One time, my brothers had constructed peashooter blowguns out of ten-inch pieces of aluminum arrows.

The "peashooter" was just a name, however. They actually shot blow darts.

My brothers would steal my mother's sewing needles and wrap them in electrical tape, leaving only about an eighth of an inch protruding. This was so your darts would stick to your victim. How else would you know if you got a hit? Kind of like paintballs, but with needles.

The minute the folks were gone, my brothers initiated seek-and-destroy combat between themselves. Furniture was turned over, and blankets were used to create dart-resistant bunkers.

During a skirmish on the border of the kitchen and family room, Kirby received intel that Jesse was ahead and behind a strong defilade: the couch. (He saw his toes sticking out from the side.) He decided to make a quick aerial attack before counterintelligence gave his position up.

As Kirby dove over the tipped couch in a high arc, he got off a good shot that thudded solidly into the top of Jesse's skull. However, in his excitement of the successful attack, he didn't remove the blowgun before hitting arrow first. This rammed the peashooter down his throat, punching a bullet-size hole right below his soft palate and dead center of the back of his throat, stopped only by bone. This was very bloody and painful.

A truce and ceasefire were agreed upon to render humanitarian aid. Time was of the essence now. Cleanup was conducted, and preteen medical attention was administered. They had to stop the bleeding and prevent infection.

Having seen Mom use Chloraseptic on throats, they figured that would be the cure, so they poured copious amounts down his throat. They thought that tickled a bit, as Kirby's eyes were watering a lot at that point. This was followed by different things my brothers knew cleaned things … like Windex. Apparently, that one really lit him up.

My brothers don't remember the story they came up with, but it seemed to work pretty well. My guess is mainly because the folks were getting pretty used to dealing with things like this by now.

\* \* \*

One time, Kirby set a fox trap and was in the process of finishing the set when he tripped and fell backward onto the trap. The trap activated on his butt cheek.

Since he was not strong enough to reach around behind him to release the springs, he had to pull the trap stake and waddle across some fields to the Overcast's house for assistance in removing the self-inflicted butt-cheek parasite.

\* \* \*

Kirby built a really cool three-story treehouse for us kids in a huge ancient tree. It had floors at ten, twenty, and thirty feet, respectively.

This castle also included an awesome rope swing that could be used from different levels of the treehouse to swing out over the yard. There were some platforms built in between the main levels to give you more options for a launch point.

The rope swing consisted of a single large rope and a wood board with a hole in it. The rope went through the hole, and a knot on the bottom kept the whole thing in place, effectively giving you a small seat with the rope between your legs.

The upper areas were off-limits to the younger folks. At this point, I had worked my way up to the thirty-foot section. The problem, however, was that at this height, the rope didn't go all the way to the platform. With my small stature at the time, it meant I had to jump in the air and pull the seat under myself while falling.

My brother Kirby and dad were talking below on the lawn. I was on my fifth jump or so when my legs missed the seat, and I was forced to hold on for dear life as I did a full Tarzan swing to the ground. I let go at the bottom of the arc, did a full face-plant, and dug a trench in the grass like a meteorite, stopping comically at the feet of my dad and brother.

While the only injury was my pride, the wind got knocked out of all of us apparently: I couldn't breathe due to the epic impact, and they couldn't breathe due to laughing.

* * *

When Kody was thirteen, he decided he could borrow the old green Forest Service pickup, which we hauled water with, and take a buddy back home after baseball practice. After all, Dad wasn't home, and the friend only lived a half mile down the road.

He was going a little too fast when he hit the washboard section near a curve, and the truck bounced and rolled over the edge down into a creek.

Both occupants were thrown from the vehicle as it rolled, and while his friend was unharmed, Kody ended up under the roof of the cab of the truck, pressed down into a muddy beaver run.

He was able to eventually crawl out from under the truck. By the grace of God, he escaped with only cuts, bruises, and a broken collarbone. They were able to go for help and the authorities were involved.

The judge told my brother he would have suspended his driver's license, but he wasn't old enough to have one. The judge ordered some small amount of community service.

His probation officer was our neighbor, who effectively gave control over the community service to my father, who had my brother wear an orange jumpsuit and pick weeds along the main roads of the small town we lived in. I am fairly sure my brother did around one hundred hours of his thirty-some-odd-hour sentence. Dad always did try to use teachable moments.

Life is always hard, and sometimes we make it harder.

The End

Thank you for reading this book and sharing in some of our stories, adventures, laughs, and lessons.

If you enjoyed this book, please tell your friends and family. That's who this book is for.

—The Gilge Family

# Acknowledgments

First and foremost, I must thank my wonderful wife, Juletta Gilge. Without her support and understanding, this book would not have happened. You win ... for a while.

I would like to thank my entire family, but especially my father, Kent Gilge. This book is about you and for you, after all. My biggest wish is that this book helps preserve some stories and hopefully inspires the next generation of Gilges to push onward.

A big thank-you to Ken and Dawn Overcast for everything they have ever done for us. When I started writing this book, I asked Kenny for advice since he has published quite a few books, and he told me, "You need to find a good editor, someone who will tell it to you straight, and preferably doesn't even like you, so that they give you the hard truths."

That made sense to me, so I asked him, "Who edited your book? Maybe I could reach out to them?"

"Well, my wife, Dawn, edited all of my books."

Good advice indeed, Kenny, someone who doesn't even like you, like your own wife...

A large shout-out to Will Tyler, who edited this book twice for me. He took it from random scribbles and notes in broken English and transformed it into what you have read today. I couldn't have done this without you, Will. You are a good friend in my book, literally...

If you are in need of a good editor, please check out TylerEditorial.com.

Last but not least, I would like to thank you ... yes, you, the reader.

What are stories if they are not shared? What is life if not lessons?

One cannot love without loss, and one cannot write without readers.

Thank you for taking the time to read this far. Share a laugh with someone new, they most likely need it more than anyone knows.